President
GEORGE WASHINGTON

by Kathy Allen
illustrated by Len Ebert

Picture Window Books
Minneapolis, Minnesota

Special thanks to our advisers for their expertise:
Susanna Robbins, M.A.
Former Assistant Editor, OAH Magazine of History

Terry Flaherty, Ph.D., Professor of English
Minnesota State University, Mankato

Editor: Jill Kalz
Designer: Abbey Fitzgerald
Page Production: Melissa Kes
Art Director: Nathan Gassman
Editorial Director: Nick Healy
Creative Director: Joe Ewest
The illustrations in this book were created with colored inks and colored pencils.

Photo Credits: cover (leather texture), Shutterstock/Leigh Prather; 2, 14, 22–23
(parchment texture), Shutterstock/AGA; 15, National Archives and Records Administration

Picture Window Books
151 Good Counsel Drive
P.O. Box 669
Mankato, MN 56002-0669
877-845-8392
www.picturewindowbooks.com

Printed in the United States of America.

All books published by Picture Window Books
are manufactured with paper containing at least
10 percent post-consumer waste.

Library of Congress Cataloging-in-Publication Data
Allen, Kathy.
President George Washington / by Kathy Allen ; illustrated by Len Ebert.
p. cm. — (Our American story)
Includes index.
ISBN 978-1-4048-5539-7 (library binding)
1. Washington, George, 1732–1799—Juvenile literature. 2. Presidents—
United States—Biography—Juvenile literature. I. Ebert, Len. II. Title.
E312.66.A47 2010
973.4'1092—dc22
[B]   2009006894

George Washington and his soldiers had few big guns. They had little training. Their food supply was small. But the Colonists wanted to break away from Great Britain. They wanted to live in a free country.

The year was 1775. The Revolutionary War had begun!

George was a careful leader. He planned well. He took the British troops by surprise when he could.

George and his brave men fought for many months. On Christmas Day, 1776, they crossed the icy Delaware River. The next day, they fought at Trenton, New Jersey, and won.

But the war was not easy. The Colonists fought through long, cold winters. Some men had no shoes. They marched barefoot through the snow.

They hoped George would lead them to victory.

Most of the fighting ended on October 19, 1781. On that day, the British troops surrendered. The Colonists had won.

A peace agreement was signed in 1783. George and his men were heroes. The United States was a free country.

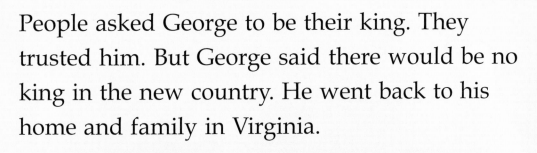

People asked George to be their king. They trusted him. But George said there would be no king in the new country. He went back to his home and family in Virginia.

However, the United States would soon need his help again.

By 1787, the United States was in danger. It owed money from the war. And there was no one to lead the states as one country.

In late May, George went back to Philadelphia
to meet with state leaders about these problems.

George and more than 50 other men talked about many good ideas and bad ideas. They argued. They went on meeting for months.

In the end, the men agreed. They wrote an important document called the U.S. Constitution. The document created a new government for the United States.

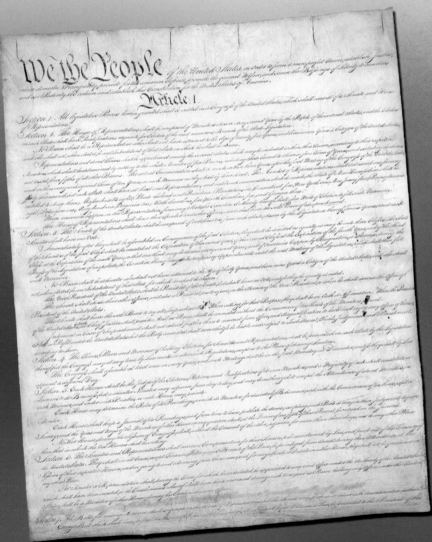

But there was still work to do. The men needed to choose a leader for the new government. George had been a strong leader before, during, and after the war. All the men chose him.

George Washington became the first president
of the United States on April 30, 1789.

At the time, New York City was the capital of the United States. George traveled there to work.

People in every city and town along the way came out to see him pass.

George chose a number of talented men to help him do his work. This group was called the cabinet.

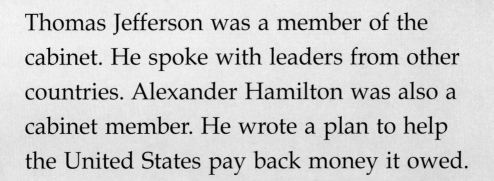

Thomas Jefferson was a member of the cabinet. He spoke with leaders from other countries. Alexander Hamilton was also a cabinet member. He wrote a plan to help the United States pay back money it owed.

George and the new government did a lot of work in a short time. They created the Bill of Rights. This document explains the freedoms of all Americans.

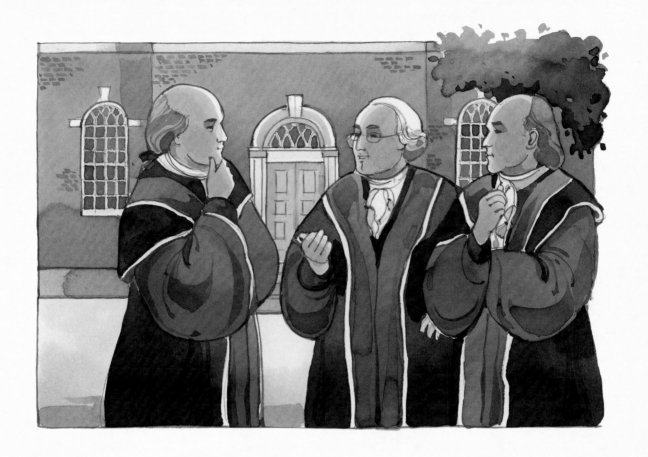

They also created the Supreme Court. The Supreme Court makes sure U.S. laws follow the Constitution.

Members of George's cabinet argued a lot. But George listened to all sides. In the end, they solved their problems in peace.

Finally, in 1797, George returned to his home and family in Virginia. He had led the United States for eight years. Now a new president led the country.

A new capital stood beside the Potomac River, too. It was called Washington, after George Washington.

Today, visitors from around the world visit the Washington Monument. They remember the first U.S. president.

A Revolutionary War soldier once wrote that George was "first in war, first in peace, and first in the hearts of his countrymen." Many people call George Washington the father of our country.

Timeline

1732	— George Washington is born in Virginia on February 22.
1775	— The Revolutionary War begins.
1783	— The Revolutionary War ends.
1787–1788	— The U.S. Constitution is approved.
1789	— George becomes the first president of the United States on April 30. He serves for eight years.
1799	— George dies at Mount Vernon on December 14 at the age of 67.

Glossary

cabinet—a group of people who give advice to the leader of a country

Colonists—the people who lived in the 13 British colonies that later became the United States

document—a piece of paper that contains important information

monument—a statue, building, or other object made to honor a person or event

Revolutionary War—(1775–1783) the American colonies' fight against Great Britain for freedom

surrendered—gave up

troops—soldiers

U.S. Constitution—a document that explains how the U.S. government works and the rules it must follow; includes the Bill of Rights, a list of freedoms all U.S. citizens have

To Learn More

∽ **More Books to Read** ∽

⇀Doeden, Matt. *George Washington: Leading a New Nation.* Mankato, Minn.: Capstone Press, 2006.

⇀Mayer, Cassie. *George Washington.* Chicago: Heinemann, 2008.

⇀Nelson, Robin. *George Washington: A Life of Leadership.* Minneapolis: Lerner, 2006.

∽ **Internet Sites** ∽

FactHound offers a safe, fun way to find Internet sites related to this book. All of the sites on FactHound have been researched by our staff.

Here's all you do:

Visit *www.facthound.com*

FactHound will fetch the best sites for you!

Look for all of the books in the Our American Story series:

⇀The First American Flag

⇀Paul Revere's Ride

⇀President George Washington

⇀Writing the U.S. Constitution